Peanuts

Trace Taylor

These are peanuts.

We love to eat peanuts.

Peanuts are seeds.

We put the peanuts in the ground.

5

Peanuts grow on plants.

6

Then lots of peanuts
come from the plants.

7

We take the peanuts.

Peanuts come in shells.

Here are peanuts in a shell.

We get the peanuts out of
the shell to eat them.

This is peanut butter.

We make peanut butter from peanuts.

13

We can make peanut
butter like this.

14

And we can make peanut butter like this.

We eat it on crackers.

We like it with bananas.

We can make cookies
with peanut butter.

We love to eat peanut butter with jelly.

19

Or we can eat it with a spoon.

We love it with chocolate, too.

Where Peanuts Are Grown

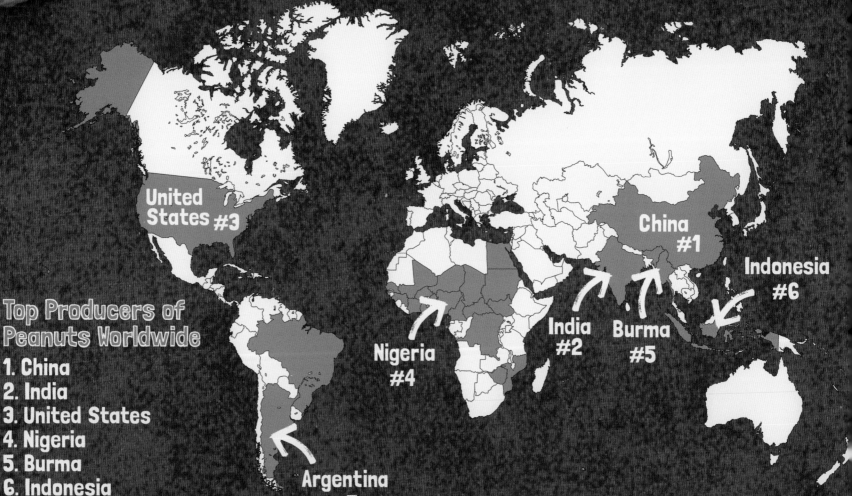

Top Producers of
Peanuts Worldwide

1. China
2. India
3. United States
4. Nigeria
5. Burma
6. Indonesia
7. Argentina

United States #3

China #1

Indonesia #6

Nigeria #4

India #2

Burma #5

Argentina #7

☐ = Peanuts

George Washington Carver

George Washington Carver was an American scientist, botanist, educator, and inventor. Carver is best known for his discovery of the many uses for peanuts. In the early 1900s, Carver helped struggling farmers by showing them peanuts as a crop to grow, use, and sell. Carver made over 100 recipes using peanuts. He even created over 100 products made from peanuts, such as cosmetics, plastic, dyes, paint, and gasoline. He was given many awards for his contributions to science and farming.

Power Words

How many can you read?

a	eat	is	make	put	these	too
and	from	it	of	take	this	we
are	get	like	on	the	to	with
can	here	lots	or	them		
come	in	love	out	then		